For the first time ever, I
Capturing a soul in motion...
being true to who I really am...
human spirit...
to learn... and expand.

Soul Catcher

a journal to help you
become who you really are

by Kathy and Amy Eldon

Acknowledgments

With gratitude to Allison Arieff,
Debra Lande, Liz Miranda, and
Michelle Barnes for catching
our ideas and turning them into
a book with soul.

Dedication

We dedicate this book to all
who yearn to be more.

Library of Congress Cataloging-in-Publication
Data available.
ISBN: 0-8118-2194-3
Printed in Hong Kong

Design and Art Direction: Liz Miranda
Illustrations: Michelle Barnes
Cover calligraphy: Alethea Morrison

Distributed in Canada by
Raincoast Books
8680 Cambie Street
Vancouver, B.C. V6P 6M9

10 9 8 7 6 5 4 3 2 1

Chronicle Books
85 Second Street
San Francisco, CA 94105
www.chroniclebooks.com

What is Soul Catcher?

Soul Catcher is a guided journal which will help you become who you really are. Through a series of questions, charts and guided artwork you will be able to identify and work through what makes you feel worried, frightened, angry, sad or happy.

Soul Catcher will guide you to access your dreams and wishes, and it will help you to find ways to break through barriers and overcome any blockages which stand in your way. It will assist you to hear the wisdom of your **inner voice,** and will support you as you define for yourself your **own true purpose**, and live the life of your choice.

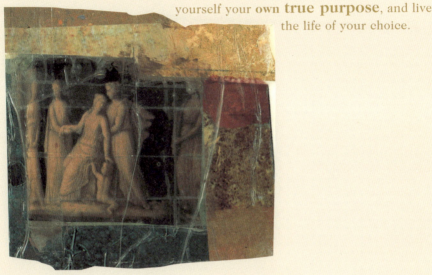

there are no rules

live the life of your choice

How to use Soul Catcher

There are no rules for using **Soul Catcher**. It's your journal, and you should feel free to use it as you wish. Sometimes you will feel like writing in it, other times, just reading the questions or quotes may help trigger a thought or memory as you work through issues and find solutions to challenges you face.

If you want, you can start at the beginning with "History of Myself," which provides charts, graphs and questions to help you create a picture of how you became the person you are. Or you can choose a chapter which relates to what's happening in your life, like "Fears and Worries" or "Pain and Loss" if you are hurting inside. Go to "Anger and Depression" if you're grappling with irate feelings which need to be dealt with (you can even throw the book against the wall if it helps!) or refer to "Jealousy and Obsession" if you need to explore darker aspects of your being and find alternatives to self-destructive behavior. Turn to "Love" if you are hoping for, or in the midst of, a love relationship. The chapter on "Dreams and Wishes" will help you put into words ideas which now may only feel like vague longings. Our chapter on "Purpose" will inspire you to identify and heed the call of your inner voice and our final chapter, "Peace and Joy" will help you celebrate when you are truly living in the flow of life.

Our questions are designed to stimulate your thoughts and feelings. If you don't like what's written, paste a sheet of paper on top and ask your own questions. Tailor the journal to your own needs: cut out articles or quotes and save letters or clippings in an envelope and place it in the back of the book. Rip out pages you don't want anyone else to read and tape the thoughts you really need to heed on your refrigerator.

Try to doodle or draw throughout the book. One of the most powerful ways to get into inner feelings is through the subconscious mind, which means scribbles and drawings are extremely useful in helping you figure out how you feel about your life. Map out your future on paper and make the plans which will transform your ideas into reality. Do this by creating collages of your wildest dreams from photographs, clippings, quotes and old greeting cards. Using these simple forms of art therapy can help you reclaim parts of yourself which may have been hidden for years. Your drawings can help heal deep inner wounds which may have caused destructive and self-defeating behavior. Don't hold back. Never use the words, "I can't, I'm not a good artist!"

As you work, take the time to be still and listen inside. You have an inner voice which is your best teacher. Encourage that voice to speak loudly and clearly. As you begin to heed the wisdom of your soul, you'll see possibilities you never could have imagined. Your spirit will soar, your energy will be uncontained and your heart will sing.

Laugh as much as possible. Toss caution to the wind, take risks with your heart, find the goodness in others and allow yourself to create the life of your choice. In the words of Cat Stevens: "You're only dancing on this earth for a short time. . ." So dance your dance loudly, dance it proudly. Dance with great joy and courage—and most of all, dance it with love!

Introduction

Within each individual lies extraordinary potential—if only we discover and accept who we really are.
***Soul Catcher** will help you do just that.*

The journal will be unique for every person, for you are the one who creates it. **Soul Catcher** provides a framework for you to examine your own life: to uncover what has shaped you in the past, to reveal what is influencing you in the present and most importantly, to ask questions that will help you consciously create the life of your choice in the future.

Keeping a journal is a magical process, allowing a gradual peeling back of the layers we have built up over the years to protect and shield our true selves. Like the body, the soul yearns for fresh air and light. By opening and exposing the inner-most regions of our spirit, we can cleanse and heal the wounds of the past, while nurturing our minds and hearts to grow and expand in the years ahead.

uncover what has shaped you

I speak from experience, having kept journals since I was a small child. I was ten when I received my first diary, a green fake leather book complete with a gold key. I diligently filled the pages with what I had for lunch, who I sat next to in Language Arts, and how my knees turned to jelly when, aged 13, I danced "close" with Leslie, the minister's son, to a bad recording of "Moon River" at a Methodist Youth Fellowship dance.

Over the years, I recorded a variety of emotions in my diary, fear and excitement at becoming an exchange student in South Africa, 10,000 miles from my high school friends in Iowa; the apprehension of my freshman year in college "out east"; and the exhilaration of sailing, at 23, with Mike Eldon, my new English husband, on the S.S. *France* to a new life in a one-room studio apartment in London.

My entries were sparse during the next few years, as I grew busy teaching art, writing children's books and looking after Dan, born in 1970, and Amy, who arrived four years later. In 1977, I started a fresh journal when our family moved to Kenya, where I plunged into an exciting career as a journalist and writer. Over the next nine years, my public writing proliferated, while my private words grew more tortured, skirting around a mysterious black hole growing inside me. It seemed that confronting the void was far too terrifying a prospect to contemplate. I managed to self-destruct in a variety of ways, and suffered the shame and humiliation of a closet bulimic. Eventually, the pain became too great and one horrible day in 1988, I left my home and family, taking with me only a brass sun god and my collection of battered journals. Alone and despairing, I left all that I cherished to embark on a journey to retrieve my soul. It was the beginning of a voyage of discovery which was nearly to kill me.

First, I traveled to the site of the ancient Oracle of Delphi in Greece, where I tried to make sense of the words which had been inscribed above the entrance: "Know Thyself". Confused, though inspired by the message of Delphi, I began to tear away at what I had allowed to become a straight jacket around my soul, isolating and restraining me from the knowledge of who I really was.

During the next three years, I underwent a deeply distressing divorce and nearly died of a debilitating disease. I moved from my beloved home and family in Africa to a small apartment in London, and from there on to California, each time uprooting myself from my friends, my possessions and my livelihood. Often during that time, I was terrified to the point of paralysis. I sought guidance wherever I could find it: through books, teachers, guides, mentors, anyone who could help me find purpose in a world which had lost its meaning. For a long time, guilt, shame, regret, fear and anger were my only traveling companions. There were many days when I didn't want to live.

Throughout that difficult period my journals sustained me as I filled book after book with clippings, articles, sayings and illustrations. I created my own primitive form of art therapy, drawing pictures of a woman slowly emerging from what was most certainly a major breakdown. At first she floated on the page, disconnected and ungrounded. One day I managed to draw her standing upright with her feet planted firmly on the ground. In time, my woman began to walk and relate to other figures. Finally, in June of 1993, five years after I left Africa, I painted a circle of dancing women on a wall in my London apartment. A few weeks later I returned to my journal to draw one more figure of "my" woman. This time her arms were outstretched as she ascended into a clear sky, smiling. I was joyous, knowing that I was in control of my life, looking ahead to a positive future ahead.

Two weeks later, my life was shattered when my son Dan, a 22-year-old Reuters photographer, was stoned to death by an angry mob in Somalia. Tormented by guilt, rage and overwhelming grief, I plummeted back into the swirling tunnel of darkness I knew so well. Again, I turned to my journals, filling whole books with anguished writings and harsh crimson and black drawings of mourning. Once more, my journals provided me with a source of comfort as I released the feelings buried deeply within; recorded poetry and writings of those who had grieved before me, and struggled with the true meaning of what had happened.

Amy, who was 18 when Dan was killed, gave me my main reason to carry on living. Separated by a continent, we passed our pain back and forth. When she was weeping, I comforted her. When I despaired, she gave me hope. Together, we began to look for ways to transform Dan's terrible death into something which would commemorate his wonderful life. We helped Mike Eldon found a center for young people in Kenya called the DEPOT, the Dan

slowly emerging

Eldon Place of Tomorrow. Amy and I began to speak out about the dangers faced by journalists and photographers, and the role of the individual in helping shift global consciousness towards compassion and understanding. Our voices became stronger, our direction more clear. We began to heal. We survived yet another journey through that long dark tunnel, to emerge, blinking in the light.

But this time, I did more than just survive. As I grew more confident I began to envision a life where I could truly live the message of Delphi—to know myself fully, and to be true to the essence of who I am. Getting to that truth has not been easy. Often, overwhelmed by the solitude of the journey and fearful of the consequences, I was overwhelmed by the immensity of the challenge.

But now, five years after Dan's death, I feel more alive and more peaceful than ever before. I have plumbed the depths of my sorrow, and I have risen to the greatest heights of joy. I have gone beyond the searing pain of loss to celebrate Dan's memory, and I have created a life filled with exciting new adventures.

I have learned that bad things happen to everyone. We get sick. Houses burn down and we suffer accidents and injuries. The people we love leave us; our children don't always understand us and we don't get along with our parents. Often people hurt us and sometimes they die. Jobs collapse, we sink into depression and lose faith in ourselves. We eat too much, drink too much and are destructive to ourselves and others. But despite all the difficult, dreadful times we endure, the human spirit always endeavors to rise above sorrow, to regenerate, to grow and expand; to learn to dance again, and one day, even to fly.

I now know that there is more to us than I had ever imagine—more than our physical beings, more than bodies and our minds. Each one of us possesses a soul, and our souls are connected. We exist in what I describe as the forces of Love, Power and Energy. You might describe the energy as God, Higher Consciousness, Source or Great Spirit. Call it what you like, it doesn't really matter as long as you use it to create the life of your choice.

Amy and I wrote **Soul Catcher** to help people do more than "just survive." We have drawn on our own experiences as well as the wisdom of a myriad of mentors and guides to create a book of questions and quotes which we hope will inspire you to venture into the unknown realms of your spirit. We ask you to become a visionary for your own life: to see beyond the ordinary; to live your dreams and follow your true purpose. We invite you to follow the urging of the Oracle of Delphi to "know thyself" and be true to yourself as you tap into the unending source of love, power and energy which empowers, supports and connects us all.

Enjoy the journey.

Kathy Eldon

energy which empowers

to learn to dance again

Starting a journal can be a scary prospect. Use this first section to help you get used to being honest with your harshest critic—yourself. Responding to the questions on each page will help you understand people, incidents, tragedies and joys which have helped to shape you. It's a way of taking stock, knowing where you are, how you got there, and will help you create a foundation for creating the life of your choice.

You may think you can't remember anything of significance. Trigger your thoughts by browsing through family albums, reading letters or talking with old friends and family members. Find music that will bring back memories, or just sit quietly and allow yourself to be transported back in time. Try closing your eyes as you tiptoe into your first bedroom. Study the wallpaper, remember the feel of the bedspread under your fingers, the sounds outside your window, the shadows on the ceiling. Picture yourself in kindergarten, having a family meal, or alone with your first love. Listen to the words people used to define you. Re-experience how you felt at home or in school, when you were being brave, or frightened. Stand above yourself and view the times you felt on top of the world—as well as the moments when you would have preferred to disappear, never to be seen again.

Memories can be misleading. Sometimes family expectations may have reshaped what really happened into something more socially acceptable. Our own minds can do the same thing, blocking memories from our consciousness, insulating us from what really happened. Be careful when you peel away the layers created over many years. It's like picking away at a scab, exposing the wound beneath. Opening the raw flesh to air and light can help in the healing process, but it's vital to approach the process with the greatest respect. Ask for help if you feel out of control or frightened by what you learn.

History of MYSELF

Our lives are profoundly affected by our family secrets that sit like elephants in the living room. We tiptoe around the creature, pretending not to notice as it trumpets for attention. The good thing is that even if no one else in your family is prepared to acknowledge the elephant (the truth) you can. Use that knowledge to fuel your quest to become who you really are.

Your journal can be your companion on the voyage inside. Use it to open up your thoughts, your feelings, and your dreams. Don't worry if what you write and draw sometimes makes you sad. Feel what you feel. Laugh, cry, shout, even if it's just in the pages of your book. Live fully in the awareness that the journey is truly the destination.

Memories

My very first memory is

I have tried to forget

I wish I could remember

About Myself

I love

I hate

I feel

I can't feel

I would like to feel

Evolution of Myself

Create your own family tree. Under the name of each person, write a list of his or her characteristics, both positive and negative. See how traits are passed on through generations. When it comes to you, figure out which qualities you wish to hang on to, and which you wish to lose.

Grandmother   Grandfather   Grandmother   Grandfather

                     Mother   Father

                     Me   Siblings

Qualities I want to develop   Qualities I want to lose

Me and Others

These people are important in my life. Some for good reasons, others not so good.

Name   Relationship   Aspects of our relationship we need to improve

Chameleons

I keep changing myself depending on who I am with. Sometimes I forget who I really am.

When I am with   I am

When I am with   I am

When I am with   I am

Who makes me feel best? Can I spend more time with that person?

Who makes me feel worst? Why do I spend time with that person?

How can I be myself all the time? I will begin by

*One of the most important results you
can bring into the world
Is the you that you really want to be.
— Robert Fritz*

If it is true that we are mirrors for one another then the qualities I most like
are reflected in me. . .and the qualities I least like in others are those I
don't like in me.

I admire

The qualities I most admire are

I don't like

The qualities which most annoy me are

What does that say about who I am?

Reviews

Compliments I have received

Horrible things people have said about me that I can't get out of my head

Why is it so much easier to remember and believe the bad things people say?

I must remember the good qualities. I am

As Others See Me

I wish I could see myself as others see me (or maybe I don't).

If I could, I would see

Here's what I need to do so others will see me as I want to be

Inspiration

I am inspired by

because

Qualities I would like to emulate

I inspire others because

inspire: to infuse into, as if by breathing:
to affect as with a supernatural influence:
to give inspiration to: to enliven.

Aspects of my life. How content I am on a scale of 0-10? How can I get to 10?

social

intellectual

emotional

physical

spiritual

career

relationship

friends

family

money

security

Words of Wisdom

Words of wisdom that have stuck in my head

Have they helped shape who I am?

Out with the Old, In with the New

I have outgrown

I miss

I don't miss

I am not quite ready for

I look forward to

Man cannot discover new oceans
until he has courage to lose sight of the sea.
— Anonymous

Worries consume us. Fears paralyze us. Anxieties, real or imagined, tear away at our confidence, rendering us powerless, afraid even to dream.

Decisions can turn us inside out. "Will I get accepted into college? Will I find a job I am passionate about? Will I ever meet someone to share my life with? Will I ever be happy in my skin? Can I survive this relationship?" There are things which seem bigger than our ability to handle them. "My child is ill. My mind hurts. I am growing old. I am frightened."

When I wake up, trembling, at 5:00 in the morning, I write about the nameless swirling around in my head by writing them all down in my journal. Next to each fear, I write down the very worst thing that can happen—then I look for solutions. Unfortunately, not all our problems have solutions.

Fears and worries

At that point, we have a choice. We can become obsessed by our worries, or we can accept that we don't have all the answers. Sometimes the truth lies in seeking a connection with God, the energy force which surrounds us all. We can surrender our fears to that Power, trusting that life is working as it should, and that in every crisis is an opportunity for growth.

Some of the most profound words on the nature of fear were spoken by Nelson Mandela, who, after spending 27 years in prison fighting apartheid in South Africa, was elected to be the President of his country. At his inauguration he said, "Our deepest fear is not that we are inadequate. Our deepest fear is that we are powerful beyond measure. It is our light, not our darkness that most frightens us." We ask ourselves, who am I to be brilliant, gorgeous, talented and fabulous?

You are a child of God. Your playing small doesn't serve the world. There's nothing enlightened about shrinking so other people won't feel insecure around you.

We are born to make manifest the glory of God that is within us. It's not just in some of us; it's in everyone. And as we let our own light shine, we unconsciously give other people permission to do the same. As we are liberated from our own fear, our presence automatically liberates others.

We all get scared, but the people who really accomplish things have learned to recognize their fears and continue on with their lives. Long ago I taught my children the song from the "King and I" which starts with "Make believe you're brave, and the trick will take you far. You may be as brave as you make believe you are." Sometimes we have to pretend we have courage in order to get through difficult times.

Use your fears as stepping stones and don't be afraid to let your light shine brilliantly as you liberate your own true self from the darkness of fear and self-doubting.

Fears

My greatest fear is

The very worst thing that can happen is

I think my fear came from

To conquer my fear I must

Could the time I spend worrying about things that may or may not happen be better spent? Instead of worrying I will

What Goes Up Must Come Down

Just when I think I'm feeling secure, something happens.

Here's how I feel now

This is how I'd like to feel

This is what I need to do to feel that way

Map of my Head

Show how much of your mind is taken by each aspect of your being:
relationship, career, money worries, family, hobbies, addictions, physical
well-being, spiritual development, creativity.

I need to spend more time on

In order to become more balanced I will

I need help.

I can call

I can write

I can get assistance by

I have access to friends, counseling services, religious leaders,
mentors, professional associations, family, help lines. . . .

1.

2.

3.

4.

Conquering Fear

They say you should "feel the fear and do it anyway." If I did that, here's what might happen

Is that okay?

Can I do it?

I will begin by

The only thing we have to fear
is fear itself.
— *Franklin Delano Roosevelt*

I can't be myself around

I think it's because

How can I come out of my shell?

Here's what I am going to do FIRST

Worry List

I am consumed with worrying.

My biggest fears are

Here are the small worries

I will conquer them by

I can't sleep.

What keeps me awake is

I need to

To find peace I will

and now I will go to sleep. . .

Bullies

I feel bullied by

I think it's because

Sometimes I bully

I think it's because

How can I handle these situations in other, more positive ways?

Here's a technique to deal with the bullies in your life. Close your eyes for a moment, and imagine them as little kids, complete with runny noses, scuffed shoes, and messy hair. Then open your eyes and realize that the person in front of you is a child inside, probably more scared of you and your power than you are of him or her.

Here's how   looks as a six-year-old!

I know there are places where I can get help, but I hate the idea of anyone knowing what is going on.

What's the worst thing that could happen if I do tell someone?

What's the best thing that could happen?

The Unknown

I fear the unknown.

For me, that means

Maybe if I learn more about it, I won't be so scared.

I will begin to overcome my fears by

If you do what you've always done
You'll get what you've always gotten.
— Anonymous

Must Do

I don't always like doing it, but I've got to

Organize my closet

Clean my desk

Go to the doctor

Visit the dentist

Write thank-you notes

He who has begun his task
has half done it.
— Horace

It's okay to be angry. It's normal sometimes to feel hurt and upset, betrayed or rejected. What's not okay is to let your anger devour you or leave you feeling dejected, depressed, powerless, devoid of energy and hope.

Some of us fear anger and deny depression. We retreat from our emotions, terrified of feeling so much. It's usually healthier to have a quick scream in the privacy of your bedroom, than to hide away all your feelings—concealing true feelings can lead to self-destructive behavior. I used to swallow my anger, gobbling it up in ice cream and candy, cookies and cake. I smiled all the time, while bingeing in private, hating myself. I didn't know how to communicate my feelings, how to say what I felt, without laying the responsibility on someone else, or taking all the blame myself.

Depression isolates us, cuts us off from those we love, and those who would love us. It surrounds, protects and cocoons us. Depression is our clue that things aren't right inside. It's a call to evaluate our lives to change our direction or perspective, a clear message that we are not in alignment with our soul's true purpose.

Anger and depression

When we are depressed or angry, we have several choices to keep from hurting so much. One is to medicate the depression with Prozac or suppress it with drugs, alcohol or food and hope it will go away. Another is to go into the pain, feel it, experience it, allow it to express itself, and use our feelings as a catalyst for change. We must ask for the help we need to find positive solutions to the problems we face. In other words, we must take control of our lives.

When you feel angry or depressed, it's time to listen inside. Use your journal to examine what it is that's making you mad, or sad. Take your power back and use it to convert your anger or sadness into activities which will help to heal and inspire you. Walk, swim or exercise. Read books which will uplift you. Find someone you care about to share a meal, or go for a hike. Plant a window box, befriend a child, visit someone who is worse off than you are. Get spiritual, medical or psychological help. Reach out to others as you face the darkness within.

Know that the world is your mirror and what you project is what you will receive. If you are angry, chances are you will live in an angry world. If you stay depressed, accepting yourself as a powerless person, you will attract other depressed, powerless people.

Use your depression as a call to transform your self. Remember your hopes and dreams and use them as you become the person you are meant to be.

Temper Tantrums

Sometimes I wish I were two years old again so I could get away with stamping my feet and pounding my fists on the floor.

The next best thing to do right now is to

Or I could

The next time I get REALLY mad I will

Teach us to care and not to care
Teach us to sit still.
       — *T.S. Eliot*

Crashing

I'm crashing today.

The problem is

Here's what I can do about it

All men's miseries derive from not being able to sit quiet in a room alone.
— *Blaise Pascal*

Betrayal

I feel betrayed.

It happened like this

In response I want to

Instead I will

Darkness

I have a dark side.

When it emerges I feel

I think it is telling me

To pass through the darkness I need to

I will begin by

If I feel myself overwhelmed again, I will

Outcast

I hate feeling rejected.

My first memory of being left out is

The worst rejection I ever felt was

My most recent rejection was

It made me feel

Is there a pattern to this? How can I change it?

How can I feel better about me?

Trust

I don't trust anyone right now not even myself.

I think it's because

In order to start trusting again, I need to

I will begin by

*In solitude alone can be known
true freedom.*
— *Michael de Montaigne*

Letter of Forgiveness

Sometimes just saying "I forgive" can help to heal deep wounds.

Dear

Surrender

Okay, I give up! I can't change it, so I'll accept it.

Here's what I have to let go of

Perfect bliss grows only in the heart made tranquil.
— Hindu proverb

Balance

Be kind to yourself.

Cut back on caffeine, coffee, tea, sodas, diet drinks and alcohol.

Get a massage, preferably with scented oils.

Get into nature. Trees, water and sunshine help you feel better.

Take a long, luxurious bath surrounded by candles and music.

Walk, hike, bicycle, garden, move!

Go to a film that makes you laugh. . . or cry.

Read something that helps you make sense of what you're experiencing.

Be kind to others, too.

Goodness

I desire goodness.

I want to be surrounded by it.

In order to receive goodness I must give it

I will begin by

The World is a great mirror. It reflects back to you what you are. If you are loving, if you are friendly, if you are helpful, the World will prove loving and friendly and helpful to you. The World is what you are.
— Thomas Drier

No one wants pain, whether from illness or injury, rejection or the anguish which follows after the loss of a loved one. We grieve at the destruction of cherished possessions or when deprived of our jobs, and we mourn the betrayal of trust in another person. If we are truly alive, we cannot escape the pain of loss.

When my first love left me, I was numb. I couldn't cry enough tears to wash away my sorrow, nor could I imagine a time when life would ever seem worthwhile again. It was then that I discovered that there is a process of grieving, a route which takes us from despair to acceptance. It's a journey which is necessary if we are to heal. Sadly, many of us have been taught to bury our feelings, covering them over with a cool, calm veneer. After years of conditioning, we become fearful of being engulfed by the power of our emotions.

Getting through the pain of loss requires you to feel. This is something which can be extremely difficult for those of us who have been taught to conceal our emotions. As a small child, I was told that crying made me "look silly." So I stopped crying and found ways to protect myself from feeling too much. I ate, I smiled a lot, I ran from myself, faster and faster, and one day I crashed, bringing everyone down around me. I often wonder how different my life might have been had I known at an early age that it's okay to cry.

PAIN and loss

Use your journal to express your feelings. Don't bury them. Go through the process of mourning the loss of whatever it is you cherished. Grieve. Allow yourself to feel the shock of loss. Go ahead and express your anger and guilt about the situation, knowing that in so doing, you will move more quickly towards a place of gentle acceptance of your loss. It is only then that you will be able to find yourself at peace, able to be open again to a new kind of joy in your life.

The great film-maker, Fellini once said, "There is no ending, no beginning, only the infinite passion of life." View your loss as a gift. Though unwanted, your grieving can trigger a profound transformation in you as you learn to lead the life of your choice with tremendous passion.

Pain and Loss

I am beyond pain

I don't know what to do

I am scared

I need help

I will call

I will listen inside

Hurting

I feel sore, like an open wound.

Here's what happened

I want to get better

Here's what needs to happen

This is what I will to do to help myself heal

The soul would have no rainbow if
the eyes had no tears.
— Native American saying

Miserable

I am miserable today.

I feel

I know I must

Broken Heart

My heart is broken.

How can I mend it?

I will start by

Hearts are meant to be broken. . . open

Loss

I feel alone.

I miss

I need

To feel comforted I will

No Time to Tell You

You left before I had a chance to tell you

I am sorry I

I know I was wrong to

I really meant to

I'd like to say

Crisis

This is what has happened

To deal with it I must

I need to get help from

Missing

There's something missing in my life right now.

To fill in the gap, I need to

I will begin by

Present Tense

I need to learn to live in the present.

I can't change what has already happened.

I can't predict what lies ahead—I can only deal with this moment.

I will let go of

I will stop worrying about

Now I will enjoy

I need to do something completely different.

Today I am going to

learn to dance

plant a window box

join a health club

play with a pet

learn how to cook something wonderful

make someone a present

arrange a bouquet of flowers

One Step at a Time. . .

The journey of a thousand miles begins with one step.
— *Lao Tzu*

Seasons

To every thing there is a season

and a time to every purpose under heaven:

A time to be born, and a time to die:

A time to plant, and a time to pluck up that which is planted;

A time to kill and a time to heal;

A time to break down and a time to build up;

A time to mourn, and a time to dance;

A time to cast away stones, and a time to gather stones together;

A time to embrace, and a time to refrain from embracing;

A time to get, and a time to lose;

A time to keep and a time to cast away

A time to rend, and a time to sew;

A time to keep silence, and a time to speak;

A time to love, and a time to hate;

A time of war, and a time of peace.

Ecclesiastics, Chapter 3, verses 1-8

obsession

We're not always nice. Not always kind and thoughtful, caring or sensitive. Sometimes we can turn into "green-eyed monsters", consumed and devoured by jealousy and passion. We can lose ourselves in obsessions, minds possessed by thoughts of a person, idea or thing. Then we feel powerless, in the grasp of an evil force which inhabits our bodies and spirits.

Jealousy and obsession

Obsessions come in many forms, including food, sex, a person, drugs, adrenaline, anything that has power over us. I was obsessed by food from my early teens. Before bulimia was ever spoken about in polite company, I used food as a weapon—against myself. Swallowing my anger, I managed to keep on smiling, though confused and frustrated inside. It took me forty years to release my obsession, during which time I became a restaurant writer and cookbook editor! Once I figured out what was "eating me," I stopped being obsessive. Once I was free to express my true feelings—to get mad when I felt angry inside, to do what I knew I had to do, no matter what, I was free.

Jealousy and obsession keep us off balance, out of control, powerless and frustrated. These emotions are far from the peace and joy we crave.

When you're in the green-eyed grasp, it's difficult to imagine a route through the slimy undercurrents to fresh air and light. The obsession can be so great that you have no desire to be liberated from its power.

When you decide you want to be free, use your journal to help you work out what's really going on inside. Answer the questions honestly. Delve into your past to see which memories might be creating your reactions. Try to understand what are causing the jealousy and hurt you are experiencing. What unfulfilled needs do you have that are fueling your obsessions?

Create a safe space around you. Try not to judge yourself for your words or actions. Meditate, pray, be gentle with yourself, and those you love. Use the power of your mind and spirit to discipline your thoughts. Express your feelings lovingly. Instead of self-destructing, look inside. Reach out. Read books, or get counseling. Remember, you are in control of your thoughts. Be honest, clear and loving.

To become who you really are, you need to release yourself from anyone or thing which has power over you. You are in control of your life, the master of your own destiny.

Greener Grass

Why do I always want what I can't have?

Why do I think I can't have it?

What would happen if I really could have what I think I want?

Would I still want it? What do I need to do to get it?

This is what I will do to get what I really want

*Jealousy: that dragon which slays love
under the pretense of keeping it alive*
— *Havelock Ellis*

I don't feel nice today.

Here's what happened

Getting over it is hard.

I need to

Consumed

I am consumed by envy.

I want what I can't have

I will get over these feelings by

Green-Eyed Monster

I am possessed by jealousy.

I feel out of control.

I want to

Right now, I need to create a safe space around me so I won't do anything stupid. I will not make snap judgments. I will stand back from the situation and at it from all perspectives.

O! beware, my lord, of jealousy.
It is the green eye'd monster which doth mock
The meat it feeds on.
— William Shakespeare

New Views

Maybe my feelings of jealousy are more about me than someone else.

What is at the root of my jealousy?

Could it be that I am feeling insecure? Inadequate?

Getting mad or crazy won't help.

How can I overcome these feelings?

To help me feel better about myself I will

The jealous bring down the curse they fear upon their own heads..
— Dorothy Dix

I have a secret. It is a burden to keep it.

I feel ashamed when I

I need help

Hiding

I don't like showing my feelings.

I learned to bury my feelings when I was

To be true to myself I need to

Angry

Too often, when I am angry I

I always know when I am out of control when I start to

Instead of self-destructing, I need to look inside myself and figure out what is going on.

Next time I am angry, I will

Obsession

My mind is racing, I can't think straight.

I am obsessed by

To overcome my obsession, I know I must

What will I gain from losing this obsession?

I will begin by

Tangled Up

I am all tangled up.

I don't know where I begin or end.

I have lost my edge.

I need to find myself again.

I will begin by listening inside.

This is what I hear

The Elephant in the Living Room

In our family we never talked about

If we had, I might have learned

I resolve to

Bad Memory

I'd like to forget

I'd like to heal

I will

Shame

I feel ashamed.

I wanted to disappear when

Here's what I will do about it

I forgive myself

Advice I give but rarely follow

I. Love yourself

2. Be gentle with yourself

3.

4.

5.

6.

7

8.

9.

10.

I am going to start listening to my own advice.

We all want to be loved. Babies won't grow without love, and grown-ups shrivel up inside when deprived of it. Love sustains, nourishes, refreshes, and energizes. Whether it is the passionate love of a new relationship, the tenderness of a grown child caring for older parents, the gentleness of a well worn friendship, or the touch of a young mother's hands on her new baby, love is the highest form of expression. Love is the most powerful force in our lives.

We all want love, but all too often in life, things go awry. A child gets frustrated with her overly-protective mother, lovers strike out at each other, couples stop talking, friends fall apart. We feel unloved—and unloving. Our hearts hurt.

To be loved, we must love. To receive, we must give. Not only to others, but first to ourselves. We must cherish, value, honor, respect and love ourselves before we are able to truly love another.

If you are lacking love in any part of your life, use your journal to go inside. Work through the pages to define your fears,

Love

hopes and perception of love. Identify old patterns which may be keeping you out of healthy relationships, and try to define new boundaries to help you feel safe. Although many of us have been brought up to be selfless in our loving, it isn't wise to lose track of our own needs. After all, the word "selfless" means "less a self". Without your self, you have nothing at all to share with those you love. As you answer the questions in this book, be honest with yourself. If you can be truthful in your journal, you will find it easier to be clear with those around you.

If you are longing for passion in your life, try to remember that as much as we long for the fire and romance of a new relationship, love is in the little things. We can create an infinite flow of love around us. It is in opening our eyes to the daily mysteries of nature, in being more aware of the miracle of being alive. It is in being able to appreciate our friends, children, parents and other loved ones, both near and far away. Focus on who needs your love, even if it's expressed in a gesture, a kind word, silent prayer, card of appreciation or a phone call . . . life is precious and all too fleeting. Be generous with your loving. Give love away, and you will find it pouring back.

The power of love heals bodies and minds, but most importantly, the human spirit. As you give love to others, love yourself, heal, energize, catalyze and transform yourself into all that you are meant to be.

Unconditional Love

I want to be loved with no strings attached, just for who I am.

I need to learn to love with no strings attached.

I will start by

Give all to love;
Obey thy heart;
Friends, kindred, days,
Estate, good fame,
Plans, credit and the Muse,
Nothing refuse.
                    — Ralph Waldo Emerson

Ownership

Some people try to possess another person.

It happened to me when

I felt

If it starts to happen again I will

Love is like quicksilver in the hand
Leave the fingers open and it stays
Clutch it and it darts away.
    — Dorothy Parker

Wanting

I yearn for

I ache

I adore

I want

I need

I keep falling for the wrong person.

Sometimes it feels like the same person over and over again.

They have these characteristics in common

Next time I'll be more aware of

Soul Mate

My ideal mate would have these qualities

You can't look, you can only find.

They say you attract at your own level.

In that case, will I be happy with anyone who is attracted to me?

Am I ready to love?

If you be loved, be worthy of love.
— Ovid

Castle Walls

I am afraid to hurt again.

I have built up walls because I don't want to make myself vulnerable.

To feel safe I need to

I will begin by

Sometimes I become completely self-absorbed and forget to look around me.

I will feel better if I can give something back instead of taking all the time.

I want to give

I will begin by

I know of one duty, and that is to love.
— Albert Camus

Receiving

I feel like I do a lot of giving.

Right now, I would really like to receive.

If no one else will give it to me, I will give it to myself.

I love

I Deserve Goodness

I deserve goodness.

I deserve kindness.

I deserve joy.

I deserve happiness.

I deserve love.

I give goodness.

I give kindness.

I give joy.

I give happiness.

I give love.

Butterflies

I can't sleep. I can't eat. I can't think.

I am in love.

I always want to remember this feeling.

Here's how we met

Here's what we said

Here's what we did

Our dreams have power. As we sleep, we process the events of the day, making sense of our lives. If we can tap into our dreams, we can use them to provide insight into our subconscious minds. We can harness our dreams to help us overcome challenges in our lives, energize us and give us the wisdom we need to help us follow our own true path.

Dreams and wishes

Use your journal to help you capture your dreams. Keep your book by your bed and when you wake up, concentrate on remembering your dreams. Write down everything, even if it seems crazy. The more you write, the more you will find you can recall. Use the margins on either side of your notes to jot down your observations on what the dream means. Remember, it's almost impossible for other people to interpret your dream, because every person, event or idea within the dream has a special meaning which only you can really understand. Use your notes to help you figure out what's troubling you, what needs doing, who you need to contact. Tap into the power of your dreams to help you solve dilemmas or inspire your creativity.

You can use your dreams to answer questions. Just before you go to bed, concentrate on the questions and ask yourself for a dream which will tell you show you the answers. Don't worry if you don't get an instant all-knowing dream the next day. It may take some time. In fact, at first you may think you don't dream at all, or if you do, you can't remember anything useful. Don't give up. Keep asking the questions and be receptive to whatever comes. Eventually, you'll find you will be able to remember snippets of your dreams, then great sequences. Be a "dream tapper", utilizing the incredible resources of your mind to find new clarity in your life.

Our daydreams are just as powerful, despite the fact that most of us have been told over and over again to "stop daydreaming and get to work." Our thoughts and wishes provide the scaffolding necessary for us to create the concrete reality of our lives. Everything begins with an idea, a wish, a dream. Instead of pushing away your daydreams, use them to visualize all that you really want in your life, whether it's a new job, health, inner peace, a relationship which works, or boundless creativity. Use your imagination as the key to the world of endless possibilities around you.

Dream big dreams. Make huge wishes. (But be careful what you wish for. . . it will probably happen.) Clearly visualize all that you would like to do — and be. Focus your positive energy on your objective and be receptive to all that awaits you. In the words of the great philosopher Goethe, "Whatever you can do, or believe you can do, begin it now. Genius has boldness, power and magic in it. Begin it now!"

Dreams and Wishes

When I was little I wanted to

When I grew older I wanted to

What's stopping me?

I will

A Picture of Me

This is the way I look

This is the way I want to look

In order to get from there to here, I must

I will begin by

The View Outside

Right now, my view is

My ideal view would be

To create my perfect view I need to

I will begin by

Perfect Day

My ideal day would be like this

Morning

Afternoon

Evening

I would share it with

What's stopping me?

Dreams

I had an important dream last night

Here's what I think it means

Secret Desires

I wish I could be

I wish I could live

I wish I could leave

I wish I could create

I wish I could forget

I wish I could overcome

I wish

What if?

If I had more time, what would I do?

If I had more money, what would I do?

If I had   what would happen?

If I didn't have   what could happen?

If I could   what would it mean?

In ten years I will be   years old. My ideal me will be

In five years I will be   years old. My ideal me will be

In one year I will be   years old. My ideal me will be

In order to achieve the ideal me, I will begin by

Do What You Love

Do what you love and the money will follow.

Here's what I would like to do

Here's how I could make money doing it

What's standing in my way?

Here's how I will start

I must apologize to

I must say I love you to

I must give

I must go to

I must have

I must do

Nothing comes from doing nothing.
— William Shakespeare

Taking Risks

What's the worst thing that could happen if I take the risk?

What's the best thing that could happen if I take the risk?

Come to the edge, he said
No we are afraid
Come to the edge, he said
No, we are afraid
Come to the edge, he said
They came,
he pushed them,
they flew

— Guillaume Apollinaire

Expanding My Horizons

I want to learn more about

I want to know

I want to grow by

Creating a Vision

I have lots of hopes and dreams. One way to bring them into reality is to visualize them.

When I dream, here's what I see

In order to transform my idea into reality, I need to

A Final Thought

Let your thoughts be positive

for they will become your words.

Let your words be positive

for they will become your actions.

Let your actions be positive

for they will become your actions.

Let your actions become your values.

Let your values be positive

for they will become your destiny.

— Mahatma Gandhi

Some people seem to be born with an internal compass. It's almost like they have their own north star twinkling overhead. But for many of us, it feels like our compass has a broken needle, and our star is hidden under a permanent cloud.

If you're one of those who still hasn't quite figured out what you're meant to do "when you grow up," don't despair. You have the fun of finding out, knowing that every day ahead provides an opportunity to move in the direction of finding your own true self. Or maybe you do know what you want to do deep inside, but haven't had the courage to live the life of your choice. Maybe you aren't sure who you really are. If that's the case, you are in for an exciting adventure, because knowing who you really are, and what your purpose is is what life's all about.

Purpose

It's a quest to know ourselves, achieve our potential and lead the richest, fullest, most satisfying life we can possibly manage. It's about finding our "bliss", as Joseph Campbell describes the state of peace we find when we're on track. Once you know who you are, and what you are REALLY meant to do, then you must remain true to yourself. Don't let anyone derail you. Don't allow anyone to tell you what they think you are you meant to do, be, think or feel. You are the captain of your ship. You hold the compass.

Staying true to yourself is the hardest thing in the world. There are so many voices trying to make themselves heard; fingers pointed every which way. It's then that you have to use your inner voice—the wisdom of your higher self, your intuition, inner guide, call it what you will—to show you the way. It takes silence and solitude to be able to hear your voice clearly. For some people, meditation provides the best vehicle for creating a still space inside. For others, it may be enough to go for a long walk, to paint or draw, to listen to music, or simply sit alone in a quiet room. Whatever it takes, find a peaceful place inside you and be aware. Listen.

The voice inside will tell you the truth—your truth. Learn to rely on your inner guidance, whether it's to help you create a master plan for your life, or simply to get you through the next few minutes, hours, days or weeks.

Learn to follow your instincts. Move in the direction of that which uplifts and energizes you, away from people or activities which drain your energy and take you down. Follow your dream, no matter what anyone else says. When you and your soul are headed in the same direction, the most incredible things happen. Be open to the magical, the mystical and inexplicable. There's an old saying, "When the student is ready, the teacher appears." As you need things, ideas, people, they will turn up, exactly at the right moment in time.

If you are diverted, and you will be, try to relax. Trust that everything that happens to you, good or bad, is part of your learning, your growing. Use the hard times as a reminder of how important it is to celebrate your life, seizing each moment as precious, knowing that everything is transient, and that the key to a fulfilled life is to accept what we are given and use it as a vehicle of transformation.

Use the pages of your journal to explore, reveal, shape, refine and define your life's purpose. Then, set your sights firmly on your own star, keep your compass at hand and bravely follow the destiny you choose to create.

Taking Stock

If I take the time to think about my life, I feel

I don't want

I desire

I regret

I fear

I long for

I hate

I love

I will

I know I have an inner voice. I just don't listen to it very often, and I'm not always good at trusting what I hear.

From this moment, I promise to listen carefully and act on what I hear.

Everyone should carefully observe which way his heart draws him, and then choose that way with all his strength.
— *Hasidic saying*

Brainstorming

I have a plan.

I need

I already have

I must find

I can ask

I can write to

I can research

I can invent

I can

The next step is. . .

I just made a decision and already I am backing down.

To be true to my intention, I must

I will begin by

Never give in, never give in, never give in. . .
— Winston Churchill

Obstacles

Something is stopping me.

Why I am not doing what I want to be doing?

Am I blaming others when I should look at myself?

What's keeping me from moving forward?

Is it possible I'm the one holding me back?

Courage

I am committed to doing

The worst thing that can happen is

I will begin by

*They can
because
they think
they can*

— Virgil

So Much to Do. . . So Little Time

I don't want my ideas to disappear.

Here is a list of projects I MUST do

1.

2.

3.

4.

5.

6.

Procrastination

I hate doing

I will do anything to avoid

These are my favorite ways to procrastinate

Here's what really needs to be done NOW

Truth

Who am I—really?

What do I truly want to do?

Can I believe that I can be who I really am, and do what I really wish to do?

If not, what's stopping me?

To be true to myself, I need to

I will begin by

To be nobody but yourself
in a world which is doing its best,
night and day, to make you
everybody but yourself —
means to fight the hardest battle
which any human being can fight
and never stop fighting.
— e.e. cummings

I know why I am here.

To achieve my purpose I need to

I will begin by

If I have the belief that I can do it,
I will surely acquire the capacity to do it, even if I may
not have it at the beginning.
— Mahatma Gandhi

In the Flow

My life is working right now.

It seems like one thing flows into another effortlessly.

I want to remember how this feels.

I believe it is happening this way because

Want to make God laugh?
Tell him your plans. . .

I feel passionate about

To hold on to this feeling, I can

There is no beginning, no ending.
Only the infinite passion of life.
— Frederico Fellini

"If only I had more money . . . if only I had the right relationship . . . if only I could leave . . . if only my kids stopped fighting . . . if only I had a better job . . . if only . . . if only. . . then I would be happy!" Sound familiar? I spent years believing that true happiness lay outside myself. Buried under the chaos and confusion of my daily life, I yearned for a respite from all that was happening. I ached for peace and the possibility of joy.

It took a total breakdown of all that I had ever known and believed for me to discover that the essence of happiness comes not from what happens outside me, but how I am inside. It was an earth shattering revelation. It meant I could no longer make events, people or my upbringing responsible for my inner peace.

Think about the people you know who seem happy. Chances are they aren't the ones with the perfect anything in their lives—except maybe their attitudes. However, those rare individuals have moved from being controlled by external events and influences to being able to remain calm, centered and in balance, no matter what happens.

Bad things happen to us and to those we love. But despite all hard things that rip into our lives, we have a choice. We can choose to roll with the punches and "go with the flow", knowing that everything that happens is part of our growth, or we can flip out, hurt others, or become self-destructive and hurt ourselves.

You don't have to be a guru or a saint to achieve inner peace. You do have to work at it though. Accepting life as it comes, and trusting that you're okay, no matter what, demands learning to control your # Joy and PEACE thoughts so they don't run away with you. Wise teachers talk about living in the present, neither regretting the past, nor anticipating the future. One way to do that is to follow some sort of spiritual discipline to help you find your center and stay there. I'm still not very good at staying still for any length of time, so I try to sit quietly and listen to music, consciously calming my thoughts. Other people find a peaceful space inside by praying. You jog or knit, paint or build model airplanes. It doesn't really matter what you do as long as your mind and spirit have a chance to be at one with each other, blissfully out of the realm of self-consciousness. It's in that union that you experience real peace and true joy.

Choose to maintain harmony in your life as you take full responsibility for who you are and you who wish to be. You are responsible for every word and action which has created your present and is shaping your future. Radiate peace and joy wherever you go, knowing that what you give to others is what you will receive.

Joy!

Right now I am really happy. I want to celebrate this moment.

I am going to

call a friend

make a special meal

put flowers on the table

listen to my favorite music

smile till my cheeks hurt

Joy is a net of love by which you can catch souls.
— Mother Theresa

Adventure

I want more excitement in my life!

In my wildest dreams I

In reality I tend to

Now I want to live my dreams

Here's what I need to do

Afoot and light-hearted I take to the open road
healthy, free, the world before me,
The long brown path
leading wherever I choose.
                    — Walt Whitman

I Feel Brave

This is what I want to do

Do what you can
with what you have
where you are.
Theodore Roosevelt

Seize the Day!

I will not let this moment pass without

Enthusiasm

Enthusiasm attracts.

What am I enthusiastic about?

How can I feel more positive?

*Every great
and commanding movement
in the annals of the world
is a triumph of enthusiasm.
Nothing great was ever achieved without it.*
— *Ralph Waldo Emerson*

Celebration

I celebrate my family by

I celebrate my friends by

I celebrate my pets by

I celebrate my life by

I celebrate

I celebrate me!

Grace

I had an unexpected gift from out of the blue today.

I feel really lucky.

Here's what happened

Miracles

I would like a miracle today.

Here's what I want to have happen.

They say that miracles are a matter of perception.

Maybe my life is full of miracles, but I haven't perceived them.

Today I'll start watching.

Miracles happen to those who
believe in them.
— *Bernard Berenson*

Blessed

I know I am blessed, even if sometimes I don't like to admit it. When I compare my life to the lives of so many others in this world, I realize I have much to be grateful for.

I appreciate

I appreciate

I appreciate

And did you get what you
wanted from this life, even so?
I did.
And what did you want?
To call myself beloved,
to feel myself
beloved on the earth.
— Raymond Carver

Peace

When I am truly myself,

I find it easy to smile.

I feel joyous and enthusiastic about my life.

I know where I am going.

I feel at peace, inside and out.

Emerging

I am taking control of my life.

I am shaping my future by being true to myself in the present.

I do not fear what lies ahead.

I am free to be me.

Helpful Reading

Alberti, Robert and Emmons, Michael. **Your Perfect Right: A Guide to Assertive Living**, 1990. A book to help one develop communication skills to become more assertive.

Bass, Ellen and Davis, Laura. **The Courage to Heal**, Harper Perennial. A bible for people sexually abused as children.

Beattie, Melodie: **Codependent No More**, Harper and Row: 1978. Offers an excellent look at the issues surrounding codependency. Also see **Beyond Codependency** (Harper and Row, 1989), which includes a twelve step program to aid recovery.

Block, Claudia. **It Will Never Happen to Me**, Ballantine, 1981. A book to help the children of alcoholic parents deal with their lives.

Breathnach, Sarah Ban. **Simple Abundance: A Daybook of Comfort and Joy**, Warner Books, 1995. Gentle essays to show us how our lives can be a perfect expression of who we really are.

Caddy, Eileen. **Footprints on the Path**: Findhorn, 1987. Inspiring words by an intrepid wisdom seeker.

Campbell, Eileen. **Lively Flame, Inspirations on Love and Relationships**, The Aquarian Press, 1992. One of a series of excellent anthologies of quotations, providing useful quotes gathered from a wide variety of sources around the world.

Campbell, Joseph, with Bill Moyers. **The Power of Myth**, Doubleday. 1988. A wonderful book which teaches us how to become heroes in our own lives.

Carlson, Richard and Shield, Benjamin. **Handbook for the Heart**, Little Brown and Company, 1996. A selection of excellent short essays on love by the thirty contemporary authors.

Carlson, Richard. **Don't Sweat the Small Stuff, and It's All Small Stuff**, Hyperion 1997. A sweet and funny book which explains how to deal calmly with the stresses of life.

Chopra, Deepak. **The Seven Spiritual Laws of Success**, Amber-Allen Publishing, 1994. Wise, clear and profoundly simple, this little book says all you really need to know about how to live an authentic and harmonious life.

Gawain, Shakti. **Creative Visualization**, New World Library, 1995. The classic book on using the power of imagination to create what you want in your life.

Gawain, Shakti. **Living in the Light**, New World Library, 1997. A beginner's guide to spiritual growth which includes helpful exercises and techniques to practice.

Gibran, Kahlil. **The Prophet**, Alfred A. Knopf, 1997. A perennial favorite, written by the Lebanese poet, philosopher and artist, Kahlil Gibran, which explores all aspects of our minds and spirits.

Hay, Louise. **You Can Heal Your Life**: Hay House, Inc. 1987. An enlightening look at how to recognize and deal with mental patterns which create disease in the body.

Jampolsky. Gerald G., M.D. **Love is Letting Go of Fear**, Celestial Arts, 1979. Teaches how to release our fears and learn to live life fully.

Jeffers, Susan, Ph.D. **Feel the Fear and Do it Anyway**, Ballantine Books, 1987. A practical guide to moving from "victim" to "creator" in our lives.

Kundtz, Dr. David. **Stopping**, Conari Press, 1998. For people in a hurry who are looking for simple ways to find peace and spiritual renewal.

Porager, Dennis: **Happiness is a Serious Problem**, Regan Books, 1998: A human nature repair manual to help beat human nature and find happiness. Diagnoses problem spots and how to fix them.

St. James, Ellen. **Simplify Your Life**, Hyperion, 1994. One hundred useful tips for slowing down our lives and enjoying the things that "really matter."

Tavies, Carol. **Anger, the Misunderstood Emotion**, Touchstone Books, 1989: Covers all faces of anger and includes helpful ways to deal with anger in one's self and others.

Tannen, Deborah. **You Just Don't Understand**, Ballantine, 1990: Well researched book about how women and men communicate with each other.

Walker, Lenore. **The Battered Woman**, Harper and Row, 1979: For women abused by husbands or roman partners. Lenore Walker deals with the myths and reality of abuse, and offers options for getting out.

Williamson, Marianne. **A Return to Love**, Harper Perennial, 1996. An accessible introduction to the wisd contained in the **Course of Miracles**.